The Race to Green End

Story by Beverley Randell
Illustrations by Isabel Lowe

Once upon a time, there were two tiny toys
who lived in a Race Game box.
One was a shiny motorbike
and the other was a red bus.

One day, they thought that they would have a race.
"I can get to Green End first,"
said the shiny motorbike.
"I can race you, because I always go fast."
He threw a 6.
"Good," he said. "I can start now."
Then he threw a 5, and off he went,
down the road to The Big Oak.

The red bus tried and tried,
but she could not throw a *6*.
A *2* was no good.
A *4* was no good.

There she was, stuck at the start.
She was still waiting at Town Gate
while the shiny motorbike
threw a *3* and then a *5*,
and went racing down the road,
around the corner by Bridge Farm,
and out of sight.

Town Gate Motors

To Green End

5

The red bus still could **not** throw a 6!
The shiny motorbike laughed at her.

He threw a 6 and then a *3*,
but when he came to The Big Hill,
he was going much too fast.
He didn't notice the small stones
on the side of the road,
and he went into a skid.
Suddenly he was off the road
and lying on the grass!

He was so shaken up
that he had to miss **three** turns.

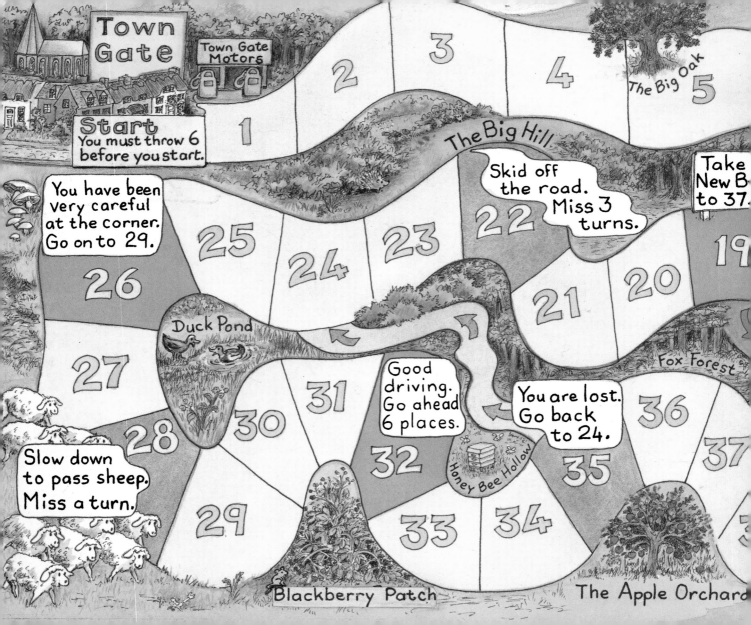

You forgot to fill up. Go back to Town Gate Motors.
Take a short cut to 16.
Bridge Farm
7
8
9
10
11
Going too fast. The police stop you. Miss a turn.
Police
16
15
You help another driver. Take another turn.
Miss a turn. Some cows are crossing the road.
12
17
14
13
You are a careful driver. Go ahead 3 places.
43
The Bad Corner. You have an accident. Go back to 40.
Motor Repairs
41
42
44
45
Miss 3 turns.
Muddy Field
46
39
40
50
Green End Picnic Place
Rabbit Hill
47
48
49
ngine is unning well. o need to stop. o on to 41.

The red bus kept on trying to throw a *6*.
She did it at last!
Then she threw a *4*, and away she went.

"I don't think that I can catch up
to the shiny motorbike now," she said,
"but I'll try." Her next throw was a *5*.
"That's good! I can go along the short cut,"
said the red bus. Then she threw a *2*.

The shiny motorbike had missed three turns,
and he looked back down the road.
The red bus was only a little way behind him!

"I'm still in front,"
said the shiny motorbike,
"I'm still winning.
I can get to Green End first.
Just watch me!"

He threw three 6s and a *4*.
Off he went, with a very loud roar.

But he was not careful enough.
When he came to The Bad Corner,
he was going too fast to get around it.
He crashed through a fence!

12

The shiny motorbike
landed upside down
in a muddy field.

His fender
was badly bent.

He had to push himself
back around the corner
to Motor Repairs
to get it fixed.

The motorbike wasn't shiny any more.
He felt sick and very sorry for himself.

Then the red bus threw a *1*.
"What **luck**!" she said. "Now I can catch up.
I'm going down New Bypass."

The shiny motorbike looked up, and he saw
the red bus coming around the corner.
He was stuck at the garage, and he knew
that he had to miss three turns, **again**!
He could only stand and watch
as the Red Bus threw a *5* and went past.

The red bus threw a *3* and a *2*.
And that was how
the tiny red bus,
who **never** tried to go fast,
got to Green End first
and won the race!

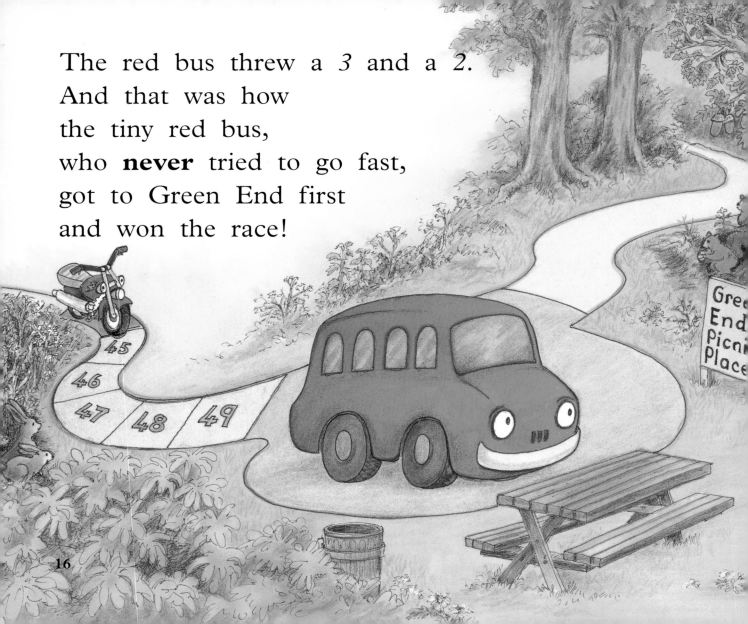

45
46
47 48 49

Gre
End
Picn
Place